"In *What on Earth Is G[...]* [...] vided a simple yet clear [...] and events in Bible prop[...] is a faithful guide for an[...] interested in getting the [...] of things to come as predicted in Bible prophecy. I recommend it highly."

DR. THOMAS ICE, EXECUTIVE DIRECTOR
PRE-TRIBULATION RESEARCH CENTER

"Dynamite comes in small packages! This little book says exactly what needs to be said about Bible prophecy and future events. It hits the nail on the head and drives home the truth about what is really happening in the world today."

DR. ED HINDSON, ASSISTANT CHANCELLOR
LIBERTY UNIVERSITY, LYNCHBURG, VIRGINIA

"…an excellent overview of our present situation in God's prophetic picture, written by a successful pastor, gifted writer, and highly respected scholar."

DR. H. L. WILLMINGTON, LIBERTY UNIVERSITY

"Mark Hitchcock's ability to communicate the complex in a concise and practical manner makes him always a delight to read. This new analysis of the most essential issues of the hour masterfully administers to people in a busy world just the right dosages of essential information and spiritual insight."

RANDALL PRICE, PH.D., PRESIDENT
WORLD OF THE BIBLE MINISTRIES, INC.

WHAT ON EARTH IS GOING ON?

MARK HITCHCOCK

Multnomah®Publishers *Sisters, Oregon*

WHAT ON EARTH IS GOING ON?
published by Multnomah Publishers, Inc.

© 2002 by Mark Hitchcock

International Standard Book Number: 1-57673-853-1

Cover design by Kirk DouPonce/UDG DesignWorks
Cover images by Getty Images
Background cover images by Corbis and Photodisc

Unless otherwise indicated, Scripture quotations are from:
New American Standard Bible® © 1960, 1977, 1995
by the Lockman Foundation. Used by permission.

Other Scripture Quotations:
Holy Bible, New Living Translation (NLT) © 1996. Used by permission
of Tyndale House Publishers, Inc. All rights reserved.

Multnomah is a trademark of Multnomah Publishers, Inc.,
and is registered in the U.S. Patent and Trademark Office.
The colophon is a trademark of Multnomah Publishers, Inc.

Printed in the United States of America

For information:
MULTNOMAH PUBLISHERS, INC.•POST OFFICE BOX 1720•SISTERS, OREGON 97759

Library of Congress Cataloging-in-Publication Data:
Hitchcock, Mark.
    What on earth is going on? / by Mark Hitchcock.
       p. cm.
Includes bibliographical references.   ISBN 1-57673-853-1 (pbk.)
    1. Bible--Prophecies--End of the world. 2. End of the world--
Biblical teaching. 3. Bible--Prophecies--Middle East. 4. Middle East--
Miscellanea. I. Title.
    BS649.E63 .H57 2002 236--dc21   2001008461

02 03 04 05 06 07 08—10 9 8 7 6 5 4 3 2 1 0

To the members of Faith Bible Church,
who were the first to hear the message of this book.
Your love for the Word and for my family
is a constant source of strength and encouragement.

For who is our hope or joy or crown of exultation?
Is it not even you, in the presence of our Lord Jesus
at His coming? For you are our glory and joy.

1 THESSALONIANS 2:19–20

CONTENTS

INTRODUCTION

One of the oldest books in the world states, "Man is born for trouble, as sparks fly upward" (Job 5:7). Never have these words been truer than today.

Twenty years ago, Billy Graham wrote these sobering yet timely words:

The whole world is sighing and suffering on a scale perhaps not known in human history: the refugees, the starving, the "new slaves," the psychological woes, the emotional turmoil, the broken marriages, the rebellious children, the terrorism and hostages, the wars, and a thousand other troubles which beset every country in the world. There are no people anywhere that are immune. The rich and famous suffer as well as the poor and obscure…. It seems that the human race may well be heading toward the climax of the tears, hurts and wounds of the centuries—Armageddon![1]

Certainly America is suffering and sighing right now—perhaps unlike ever before. World events and events close to home are a deep cause of worry and fear for many people. In recent years we have seen rioting in Los Angeles, poison gas attacks on Japanese subway commuters, disgruntled former employees on senseless shooting sprees, troubled students slaughtering their classmates, the Oklahoma City bombing, and now upward of three thousand people killed in New York City and Washington D.C. by murderous terrorists, with the continuing threat of more terrorist acts—even chemical and biological terrorism.

Recent world events have also caused people to rethink their lives and ask all kinds of questions about

God, man, life, our world, and the future. Did God cause this to happen? If God is in control, why didn't He stop this from happening? Is God judging America? Was Satan behind this? How can people be so evil? How can anything good possibly come out of this cataclysm? What's next?

Though I have heard or read all of these questions and more in the weeks and months following the terrorist attack on America, one question has emerged most frequently and persistently: Is this the end of the world? The question is asked in many different ways: Is this the beginning of the end times? Is this attack predicted in the Bible? How does this event fit into Bible prophecy? But the gist of these questions is the same: *What on earth is going on?*

I certainly don't profess to have all the answers to these questions, but I do believe that a proper understanding of what the Bible says about the end times can shed some light on how the recent events in our country fit into God's overall end-times drama.

God has not given us many of the details about the end times that we would like to know, but He has graciously given us the big picture, the blueprint of coming events. And when we see some of the major trends for the end times taking form right before our eyes, we need to wake up and pay attention.

I believe it is important for every person to understand how the events prophesied in Scripture are shaping up today. This understanding is important in order to call us to preparedness for the Lord's coming. Moreover, we need to understand the times in which we live so we will be equipped to share with others, to use the opportunities God gives us, and to seize this time when people are searching for answers to help them understand how the unfolding world events of today are important pieces in God's plan for the ages.

Someone has wisely said, "If you want to know what happened yesterday, read the newspaper; if you want to know what happened today, listen to the evening news; if you want to know what will happen tomorrow, read the Bible."

Most of us have spent a lot of time reading newspapers and watching the news in the past few months. But let's remember to read and study the Bible too, for it alone can tell us what will happen tomorrow. That's what *What on Earth Is Going On?* is all about.

In this book I am going to assume that the reader has at least a basic knowledge of events in the end times. To make sure you understand these events, let's do a brief review and define a few key terms that you will see sprinkled throughout the book.

THE RAPTURE OF THE CHURCH TO HEAVEN

This next event on God's prophetic timetable is the Rapture. This is when all people, living or dead, who have personally trusted in Jesus Christ as their Savior will be caught up in the air to meet the Lord and go with Him up to heaven and then return with Him to earth at least seven years later, at His second coming (see John 14:1–3; 1 Corinthians 15:50–58; 1 Thessalonians 4:13–18).

THE SEVEN-YEAR TRIBULATION PERIOD

The Tribulation is the final seven years of this age. It will begin with a peace treaty between Israel and the Antichrist and end with the second coming of Christ to earth (not to be confused with the Rapture).

During these seven years, the Lord will pour out His wrath upon the earth in successive waves of judgment. But the Lord will also pour out His grace during this time by saving millions of people (see Revelation 6–19).

THE THREE-AND-A-HALF-YEAR WORLD EMPIRE OF THE ANTICHRIST

In the last half of the Tribulation, the Antichrist will rule the world politically, economically, and religiously. The entire world will either give allegiance to him or suffer persecution and death (see Revelation 13:1–18).

THE CAMPAIGN OF ARMAGEDDON

The campaign or war of Armageddon is the final event of the Great Tribulation. In this war, all the armies of the earth will gather to come against Israel and attempt to eradicate the Jewish people once and for all (see Revelation 16:12–16; 19:19–21).

THE SECOND COMING
OF CHRIST TO EARTH

The climactic event of human history is the literal, physical, visible, glorious return of Jesus Christ back to planet earth to destroy the armies of the world gathered in Israel and to set up His kingdom on earth, a kingdom that will last for one thousand years (see Revelation 19:11–21).

God's Blueprint for the End Times

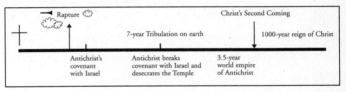

One final word to let you know where I'm coming from: I approach Bible prophecy from a premillennial, pretribulational position. That's a fancy way of saying that I believe that Jesus will come to rapture His people to heaven *before* the seven-year tribulation period and that He will return to earth at the *end* of the Tribulation to set up His thousand-year reign on earth.

You may not agree with my position or with every detail in this book. That's all right, but the main point I hope you come away with is that world news is significant to Bible prophecy and to the end times. And though Scripture does not justify setting any precise schedule for the coming of Christ, we have every reason to believe that His appearance in the air to retrieve His people could be very near.

Maranatha!
"Our Lord, Come!"
MARK HITCHCOCK

9/11

I will never forget where I was when I first heard the news of the terrorist attack on September 11, 2001. I was just getting out of my car at church when the radio announcer said that an airplane had crashed into the World Trade Center in New York City.

At first I thought that a small plane had probably gone off course or that bad weather in New York had caused the plane to accidentally hit the World Trade Center. I said a brief prayer and headed to my office.

About thirty minutes later, women started arriving for our Tuesday morning Bible study. One by one they made their way to my office, asking me if I had heard about the plane crash in New York. Then those arriving later began to say that another plane had hit the World Trade Center. A few minutes later another lady told me that a plane had hit the Pentagon. Others told me that another plane had crashed somewhere in Pennsylvania. I got a sick feeling in the pit of my stomach. It felt like I was living a nightmare.

I made my way to the nearest TV to see what was going on. When I saw the video footage of the planes hitting the World Trade Center, I couldn't believe what I was seeing. It was like something from a movie. It was like a scene from Revelation. It was nothing short of apocalyptic. I was stunned and speechless.

Just as I will never forget where I was when I first heard the news of the attack and how I felt, I will also never forget the first thing that came into my mind. I immediately thought of the words of Jesus:

"There will be signs in sun and moon and stars, and on the earth dismay among nations, in perplexity at the roaring of the sea and the waves, men fainting from fear and the expectation of the things which are coming upon the world; for the powers of the heavens will be shaken. Then they will see THE SON OF MAN COMING IN A CLOUD with power and great glory. But when these things begin to take place, straighten up and lift up your heads, because your redemption is drawing near." (Luke 21:25–28)

Jesus said that when the events of the end of the age begin to unfold, people will be overcome with fear and panic. The response of all men will be fainting and a deep, somber sense of imminent foreboding.

We all witnessed this response firsthand. People everywhere were gripped with intense, paralyzing fear and panic. You could see it deeply etched on every face. You could hear it in the voices. You could feel it in the pit of your stomach. We all kept wondering, *What's next? Where will the terror strike next?* A deep sense of fear and trepidation about the future overtook people.

All of this was by design. Fear, anxiety, disruption, and terror were the stated goals of the terrorists. That's what they're all about—terror. After the attacks, Osama bin Laden said, "America has been filled with horror from north to south and east to west, and thanks be to God."

The cover of *Time* on October 22, 2001, revealed the fragile psyche of the wounded nation. "The Fear Factor: Anthrax letters. FBI warnings. Bin Laden's videotapes. Bombarded by threats real and imagined, a nation on edge asks, What's next?"

Just between September 7 and 28, 2001, prescriptions for antianxiety drugs nationwide increased 8.6 percent. People desperately want some kind of assurance that everything is going to be okay. We want some good news. We want to hear that this is all a bad dream.

GOOD NEWS, BAD NEWS

The Bible contains the ultimate Good News. In the midst of the pessimism, gloom, and frustration of this present hour, there is one great beacon of hope: the promise of Jesus Christ. "'If I go and prepare a place for you, I will come again and receive you to Myself, that where I am, there you may be also'" (John 14:3).

This promise assures us that all who have received Jesus Christ as their personal Savior from sin will spend eternity with the Lord in heaven. And not only that, but all believers in Christ will be rescued by the Lord (raptured) from the coming Tribulation. So we can say emphatically that for those who know the Lord the best is yet to come.

But the Bible also contains some very bad news. Before Jesus returns to earth at His second coming, things are going to get bad—really bad. I wish I could say that everything is going to be okay, that everything will get better and better until Jesus comes. But the Bible says that the worst is yet to come for planet earth.

Before we get into the specifics of how current events in our world today fit into God's plan for the ages, let's look at Jesus' general forecast for the future.

THE WORST IS YET TO COME

"WORLD TRADE CENTER COLLAPSES"

"PENTAGON HIT BY FLYING BOMB"

"ANTHRAX!"

"PLASTIC EXPLOSIVES FOUND"

"THOUSANDS LAID OFF"

"RECESSION"

"SMALLPOX EPIDEMIC?"

"DOOMSDAY"

"ARMAGEDDON"

None of us ever thought we would see headlines like these. Yet they top the news with surreal regularity. The news is gloomy. Security eludes us like a phantom. The foundations of our society seem to be crumbling under our feet. Uncertainty about the future makes long-range planning next to impossible. No one seems to be able to tell us what lies ahead.

But Jesus knows, and it would be wise for us to listen to His forecast for the future. He is the only one who can accurately tell us what the future holds.

JESUS' FINAL WARNING

Jesus gave His disciples and us a general blueprint of what we should look for in the days just before His glorious return to earth.

The setting in which Jesus shared this was His farewell message to His confused band of disciples. Jesus had been with them for more than three years, and they still did not understand what was about to happen to their leader. Two days later, on Friday, He would be nailed to a Roman cross and suffer a cruel, barbaric death. But it was still Wednesday of the final week of His life, and from the Mount of Olives, a hill east of Jerusalem, Jesus was about to unveil a sweeping panorama of the future for His disciples.

Jesus and the Twelve slowly ascended the hill. The summit overlooked the temple mount in Jerusalem, two hundred feet below. Because it was Passover season, the temple precinct would have been teeming with pilgrims. When they reached the summit, Jesus seated

Himself on a rock. Soon four of the disciples—Peter, James, John, and Andrew—approached Him privately and asked a question that had probably been burning in their hearts for some time: "Tell us, when will these things happen, and what will be the sign of Your coming, and of the end of the age?" (Matthew 24:3).

Their question is one that many are still asking today: "When will the world come to an end?" As the late afternoon shadows lengthened over the city of Jerusalem, Israel's premier prophet began to paint a gloomy portrait of the end of the age. He told His followers that the worst is yet to come.[2]

HARD TIMES AHEAD

Jesus told His disciples many things in that great discourse from the Mount of Olives, but one point comes through loud and clear: This world is not going to become a better place to live in. Times of almost unbelievable difficulty are on the horizon. Jesus said that the end of the age will be a unique time of terror. Nothing in all of world history will even compare to what is coming. It will totally eclipse all previous history in terms of hardship and trouble. "For then there will be a great tribulation, such as has not occurred since the beginning of the world until now, nor ever will" (Matthew 24:21).

Now that's saying a lot, because there have been some terrible times in the past, haven't there? Plagues that wiped out millions. Bloody battles. Famines. World wars. Earthquakes. The Holocaust. What is it that will make this future time, this "Great Tribulation," so much worse than any other time in history?

Two things.

THINK GLOBALLY

The first reason the tribulation period will be the worst time in history is that the terror and destruction of it will be worldwide in scope, not just limited to a few locations. Just think about it: In the Tribulation there will be disasters of unimaginable horror and global scope.

Jesus' discourse from the Mount of Olives is often called "the mini-Apocalypse" because it gives a broad overview of the events of the end of the age. The Apocalypse itself, the book of Revelation, amplifies and fills in many of the details that Jesus did not give in His blueprint of the end times.

Revelation 6–19 is the main section of the Bible that describes the Tribulation. These fourteen chapters focus on the terrible judgments of the end times. The main events in these chapters are the three sets of seven judgments that the Lord pours out on the earth.

There are seven seal judgments (see Revelation 6), seven trumpet judgments (see Revelation 8–9), and seven bowl judgments (see Revelation 16). This series of judgments will be poured out successively during the Tribulation.

The seven seals will be opened during the first half of the Tribulation. The seven trumpets will be blown during the second half of the Tribulation. And the seven bowls will be poured out in a very brief period of time right near the end of the Tribulation, just before Christ returns.

Sequence of Judgments

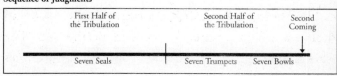

Scripture often compares these judgments to birth pangs (see Jeremiah 30:4–7; Matthew 24:8; 1 Thessalonians 5:3). Like birth pangs, as the Tribulation progresses, these judgments will irreversibly intensify in their severity and frequency.

These three crashing waves of God's judgment are described in detail in Revelation 6–19.

The Seven Seals

Seal	Symbol	Meaning	Revelation
First Seal	White Horse	Antichrist	6:1–2
Second Seal	Red Horse	War	6:3–4
Third Seal	Black Horse	Famine	6:5–6
Fourth Seal	Pale Horse	Death and hell	6:7–8
Fifth Seal	—	Martyrs in heaven	6:9–11
Sixth Seal	—	Universal upheaval and devastation	6:12–17
Seventh Seal	The Seven Trumpets	Begins next wave of judgment	8:1–2

The Seven Trumpets

Trumpet	Event	Result	Revelation
First Trumpet	Bloody hail and fire	One-third of vegetation destroyed	8:7
Second Trumpet	Fireball from heaven	One-third of oceans polluted	8:8–9
Third Trumpet	Falling star	One-third of fresh water polluted	8:10–11
Fourth Trumpet	Darkness	One-third of sun, moon, and stars darkened	8:12
Fifth Trumpet	Demonic invasion	Torment	9:1–12
Sixth Trumpet	Demonic army	One-third of mankind killed	9:13–21
Seventh Trumpet	The kingdom	The announcement	11:15–19

The Seven Bowls

It boggles the mind just to read this list. One half of the earth's population will perish in just *two* of the twenty-one judgments (see Revelation 6:8; 9:18). The entire environment of the planet will be destroyed. Revelation graphically pictures the worldwide devastation:

The cities of the nations fell.... And every island fled away, and the mountains were not found. And huge hailstones, about one hundred pounds each, came down from heaven upon men. (Revelation 16:19–21)

Just think what it would be like to live on earth while all this is transpiring.

Bowl	Poured Out	Result	Revelation
First Bowl	Upon the earth	Sores on the worshipers of the Antichrist	16:2
Second Bowl	Upon the seas	Seas turned to blood	16:3
Third Bowl	Upon the fresh water	Fresh water turned to blood	16:4–7
Fourth Bowl	Upon the sun	Intense, scorching heat	16:8–9
Fifth Bowl	Upon the Antichrist's kingdom	Darkness and pain	16:10–11
Sixth Bowl	Upon the Euphrates River	Armageddon	16:12–16
Seventh Bowl	Upon the air	Earthquake and hail	16:17–21

THE WRATH OF GOD

The second key reason why the end of the age will be by far the worst time in history is that God's wrath will be unleashed. Today, much of the suffering, destruction, and trouble we see in the world is the result of the wrath of sinful man and of Satan. But in the Tribulation, God Himself will be pouring out His wrath on a sinful, rebellious world. All twenty-one of the Tribulation judgments listed in Revelation are from the hand of the Almighty.

Sinful men will know that the worldwide judgments on the earth, seas, sun, and sky are coming from the hand of almighty God Himself. And God's wrath will be unlike anything the world has ever seen.

CALLING TO THE ROCKS

The response of terrified people during the Tribulation will be much like what we saw on September 11—but multiplied a thousand times. It will be nothing short of unmitigated terror and panic. Consider these sober words from the book of Revelation:

I looked when He broke the sixth seal, and there was a great earthquake; and the sun became black as sackcloth made of hair, and the whole moon became like blood; and the stars of the sky fell to the earth, as a fig tree casts its unripe figs when shaken by a great wind. The sky was split apart like a scroll when it is rolled up, and every mountain and island were moved out of their places. Then the kings of the earth and the great men and the commanders and the rich and the strong and every slave and free man hid themselves in the caves and among the rocks of the mountains; and they said to the mountains and to the rocks, "Fall on us and hide us from the presence of Him who sits on the throne, and from the wrath of the Lamb; for the great day of their wrath has come, and who is able to stand?" (Revelation 6:12–17)

Talk about fear. Talk about panic. When God begins to judge this sinful world during the Tribulation, there will be no place to hide. The emotional suffering will be so intense that men will long to die. They will cry out for the mountains and rocks to fall on them and end their suffering. They will even try to commit suicide, but to no avail: "And in those days men will seek death and will not find it; they will long to die, and death flees from them" (Revelation 9:6).

Charles Ryrie, a well-known theologian, vividly interprets this amazing statement:

> The effect of this torment is to drive men to suicide, but they will not be able to die. Although men will prefer death to the agony of living, death will not be possible. Bodies will not sink and drown; poisons and pills will have no effect; and somehow even bullets and knives will not do their intended job.[3]

A PREVIEW OF THINGS TO COME

As unsettling as the events in our world today have become, I believe they are only a pale preview, a faint foreshadowing of what is coming upon the whole world. The preview we are seeing now is terrible. Just think what the reality will be like. On September 11, the twin towers in New York City fell. At the end of the Tribulation, entire "cities of the nations" will fall. It's too horrible to even imagine. Yet the Bible says it's coming. But when?

That's the real question people everywhere are asking. It's the issue of the hour. Inquiring minds want to know: Are there any events on the horizon today that tell us that the end of the age could be near? Are there any signs of the end times in the world today? Are the events of September 11 and the aftermath signs of the end times?

To make sure we get off on the right foot, let's begin this important investigation by making sure that we understand what the Bible says about the signs of the times.

SIGNS OF
THE TIMES?

One evening a man stayed up late reading an engrossing novel after his wife had retired upstairs to bed. Since he didn't have his watch on, the man listened each time the grandfather clock chimed so he wouldn't stay up too late. At 10:00 P.M. it chimed ten times and at 11:00 it chimed eleven times.

As the man was about to finish the book, he heard the clock begin to chime the midnight hour. Just to make sure he hadn't missed an hour in his focus on the book, he began to count the chimes. Ten, eleven, twelve...*thirteen*. Startled, the man ran upstairs and shook his sleeping wife: "Honey, wake up—it's later than it has ever been!"

As planet earth approaches the midnight hour, one thing we know for sure: It's later than it has ever been.

But is it possible to be any more specific than this? Is it possible to see specific signs of the times that indicate the end times are near? Whenever dramatic, world-shaking events shock the world, we naturally want answers. We want to know what's happening. We want to make sense out of what often seems chaotic, disconnected, and frightening.

Everywhere a Sign

In our attempt to make sense out of world news and current events, we need to carefully avoid two extremes. The first extreme is *sensationalism*.

Sometimes in our desperation to comprehend what is happening in the world, we can become gullible and easily led astray by sensationalistic claims. Among the most egregious sensationalists are those who set dates for the coming of Christ; people who are always trying to identify the Antichrist; and those who try to make every earthquake, disease, disaster, or feud between nations a sign of the end times. For too many prophecy buffs, virtually everything that happens is a sign that the Lord's coming is near.

Unfortunately, the recent events in our nation have provided new fodder for sensationalists. In the wake of the September 11 attacks, all kinds of strange rumors began circulating.

For instance, I received a fax containing photographs of the burning, smoke-enshrouded World Trade Center Towers. If you looked closely enough at the photos, you could make out the image of a face in the smoke. And if you really looked intently, you could even see horns on the head. I had many people call to ask if I thought this was the face of Satan in the smoke.

Of course, the idea is ridiculous. First, Satan is a spiritual being—he has no physical face. Second, although Satan can assume material form, even if he chose to do so, nothing in the Bible indicates that he has horns.

Another hoax that made its way around as early as the day after the attack was that this event had been prophesied by Nostradamus, the French physician and physicist who lived in the sixteenth century. The alleged prophecy read as follows (though other versions abound):

> In the year of the new century and nine months,
> From the sky will come a great King of Terror
> The sky will burn at forty-five degrees.
> Fire approaches the great new city
>
> In the city of York there will be a great collapse,
> Two twin brothers torn apart by chaos
> While the fortress falls the great leader will succumb
> The third big war will begin when the big city is
> burning.

This got a lot of people worked up. But the whole thing turned out to be a big hoax. Nostradamus didn't predict anything close to this. While a simple version of this "prophecy" made the rounds in e-mail inboxes, embellished versions soon appeared that made it fit the events of September 11 perfectly.

I also heard that the events of September 11 fulfilled specific Bible prophecies. For instance, I heard some say that New York City is the great harlot who is destroyed in Revelation 17–18. Many people asked me if the destroyed "towers" in Zephaniah 1:16 were a reference to the World Trade Center Towers. Others have said that this is *the* "beginning of birth pangs" predicted in Matthew 24:8.

This just shows how careful we need to be in times like these. When people are searching for answers, there will always be those who offer sensational ideas that people desperately grab onto without really knowing all the facts.

We must vigilantly avoid sensationalism.

WHAT SIGNS?

Another extreme we must avoid in times like these is scoffing at the signs of the times. If sensationalism can be likened to overselling, then *scoffing* is underselling. Many today react negatively to any talk of signs of the end times. They say it is foolish and unwarranted to look for or even talk about trends and developments that point toward the end-time scenario portrayed in Scripture.

Is this negative outlook justified? Jesus sternly

rebuked the religious leaders of His day for their blindness to the signs of His first coming:

> The Pharisees and Sadducees came up, and testing Jesus, they asked Him to show them a sign from heaven. But He replied to them, "When it is evening, you say, 'It will be fair weather, for the sky is red.' And in the morning, 'There will be a storm today, for the sky is red and threatening.' Do you know how to discern the appearance of the sky, but cannot discern the signs of the times?" (Matthew 16:1–3)

Jesus was fulfilling the Old Testament prophecies and performing the prophesied miracles of the Messiah right before their eyes, yet they were blind to the clear signs of His first coming.

Likewise today, many religious leaders are following the same sad pattern of being blind to the things happening in the world that are related to God's program for the second coming of Christ.

THE LESSON OF THE FIG TREE

When Jesus' disciples asked Him what the signs of His coming and the end of the age were, He didn't say, "Don't worry about signs of the end of the age." Nor did He tell them it wasn't any of their business. No, in Matthew 24:4–31, He outlined several general and specific signs of the end of the age.

After listing some of the main signs, Jesus concluded with the parable of the fig tree in Matthew 24:32–33.

> "Now learn a lesson from the fig tree. When its buds become tender and its leaves begin to sprout, you know without being told that summer is near. Just so, when you see the events I've described beginning to happen, you can know his return is very near, right at the door." (NLT)

In the Old Testament, the fig tree was often used as a symbol for the nation of Israel, so many Bible interpreters understand this parable in that light. But I believe that Jesus is simply using a natural illustration that anyone can understand. He is saying that just as one can tell that summer is near by the blossoming of the fig tree, so those alive during the Tribulation will be able to see that His coming is near when the signs He has just listed (in Matthew 24:4–31) begin to happen.

DARK SHADOWS

When it comes to the subject of the signs of the end times, clear thinking, sensibleness, and balance are desperately needed. The rapture of the church, the next great event on God's prophetic timetable, has no signs that must precede it. This is a very important point to understand.

All the end-time prophecies in the Bible relate to the time of the seven-year tribulation period and the second coming of Christ to earth to rule and reign, not the Rapture. The Rapture is an imminent, signless event. It's an event that, as far as we know, could occur at any moment.

Therefore, what we are seeing in the world today are not signs of the Rapture, but signs of events that will occur *after the Rapture* in preparation for Jesus' second coming to earth to reign as King of kings and Lord of lords.

A few days ago I was going out to jog. I started off by walking for a few minutes to get warmed up. As I walked along the sidewalk, I noticed that my shadow was being cast on the concrete in front of me. Something about it struck me. I realized that my shadow is not me—it's not the substance—but it signals that I am not far behind. It's a sign that I am coming. In the same way, coming events often cast their shadows upon this world before they arrive. The shadows function as signs of the times.

SETTING THE STAGE

Another way to understand the signs of the times is to imagine that you're at a play. The curtain has not yet risen for act one, but from your seat in the audience you can hear sounds behind the curtain. The stage is being set for the beginning of the play. The props are being put in place and the actors are taking their positions. These events are not the play itself; they are a natural, necessary preparation for it. When we hear the stage being set, anticipation grows for the rise of the curtain.

In the same way, God has already written the

script for the end times and is preparing the world stage for His drama of the ages. The curtain is still down, but world events are taking place and actors are assuming their roles for the drama to begin. Before the curtain lifts, the church will rise in the air to meet the Lord at the Rapture. Sometime after the Rapture, the Antichrist will arrive on the world scene. At that point all the pieces and players will be in place, and the final drama of the ages will begin.

Thomas Ice and Timothy Demy, respected experts in Bible prophecy, provide an excellent summary of this view:

> Bible prophecy relates to a time after the rapture (the seven-year tribulation period). However, this does not mean that God is not preparing the world for that future time during the present church age—in fact, He is. But this is not "fulfillment" of Bible prophecy. So while prophecy is not being fulfilled in our day, it does not follow that we cannot track "general trends" in current preparation for the coming Tribulation, especially since it imme-

diately follows the rapture. We call this approach "stage setting." Just as many people set their clothes out the night before they wear them the following day, so in the same sense is God preparing the world for the certain fulfillment of prophecy in a future time.

The Bible provides detailed prophecy about the seven-year Tribulation. In fact, Revelation 4–19 gives a detailed, sequential outline of the major players and events. Using Revelation as a framework, a Bible student is able to harmonize the hundreds of other passages that speak of the seven-year Tribulation into a clear model of the next time period for planet earth. With such a template to guide us, we can see that already God is preparing or setting the stage of the world in which the great drama of the Tribulation will unfold. In this way this future time casts shadows of expectation in our own day so that current events provide discernible signs of the times.[4]

It may not be long before the world hears "Curtain!"

THE DAY IS DRAWING NEAR

On October 1, 2001, I saw a *Close to Home* cartoon that graphically makes the point of how current events can provide discernible signs of the times. The cartoon shows several people walking in the vestibule of a shopping mall with a Santa display in the center surrounded by large candy canes and wreaths. In the background, Christmas music is playing over the mall speaker system. The caption read: "With Columbus Day rapidly approaching, malls across the country scramble to set up their Christmas displays."

The second coming of Christ to earth at the end of the Tribulation is like Christmas. Many very specific signs that are outlined in Scripture will precede it. The rapture of the church is like Columbus Day. There are no specific signs of its coming. You never see decorations for Columbus Day. However, if it's fall and you already begin to see signs of Christmas everywhere, and Columbus Day has not yet arrived, then you know that Columbus Day is near.

I believe that the events of September 11, 2001, and the aftermath have had a major stage-setting effect for the coming events of the end times. On that day, I believe that a kind of prophetic "shift of gears" occurred that is accelerating the world toward its climax. The signs of "Christmas" are all around us—so the coming of Christ at the Rapture could be very soon.

In the next five chapters we'll look at five specific ways that international and domestic current events in our nation serve as signs of the times.

ISRAEL— GOD'S SUPERSIGN

In the days following September 11, one question came up over and over again: *Why?* It's the question we always ask when tragedies occur. In this case, we all wanted to know why someone would do something like that. What could possibly inspire such evil?

Many answers were given: U.S. foreign policy ("meddling") in the Middle East; Muslim bitterness over the presence of seven thousand U.S. troops ("infidels") on Muslim soil in Saudi Arabia; cultural differences between America and Muslim nations; American arrogance and prosperity; and Islamic extremists that view America as the "Great Satan" or enemy of God.

Though many of these factors no doubt contributed to the terrorists' motivation, one reason eclipses all the others: Israel.

In a *Time* article titled "Roots of Rage," Lisa Beyer gets to the source of the hatred that many Arab and Islamic nations have for America. She makes this important observation about the real cause of the hatred for America:

Certainly the greatest single source of Arab displeasure with the U.S. is its stalwart support of Israel: politically (notably at the U.N.), economically ($840 million in aid annually) and militarily ($3 billion more, plus access to advanced U.S. weapons). To a majority of Arabs, Israel, as a Jewish state, is an unwelcome, alien entity. Even to those who accept its existence, Israel is an oppressor of Arab rights; despite the Oslo peace process, it still occupies most of the Palestinian territories. Particularly egregious to Muslims is Israel's control over

Islamic shrines in Jerusalem, the third most sacred city to Islam.... When it comes time to broker peace in the region, many Arabs are inflamed by the strong U.S. bias in negotiations. To Islamic fanatics, including bin Laden, the peace process is of course anathema; for them, Israel is a state to be destroyed, not to be bargained with. Bin Laden, a Saudi, speaks out frequently against Israel.[5]

Even Saudi prince Alwaleed bin Talal brought the spotlight on Israel. He is the sixth richest man in the world, with a net worth topping $20 billion. He came to New York City shortly after the terrorist attacks to offer his condolences and a gift of $10 million to Mayor Giuliani's Twin Towers Fund. However, Giuliani flatly refused the gift when he was made aware of a statement the prince had made in conjunction with the gift. Prince Talal said that the U.S. "should reexamine its policies in the Middle East and adopt a more balanced stance toward the Palestinians."[6] He added that the U.S. should push Israel toward peace with the Arab states.

Other Saudi leaders expressed the same sentiment. Osama bin Laden, in his televised rants, made reference to the Zionist infidels and the Palestinian issue.

WHY ISRAEL?

This is truly amazing. It all comes back to Israel. Israel is the key. Why is this so amazing? Because the Bible predicts that in the end times Israel will be regathered to her land and that she will be in the world spotlight.

What's the big deal about Israel? The modern nation of Israel didn't even exist until May 1948. The entire country is only about the size of New Jersey with a total population of only about 6.3 million, 5.1 million of them Jewish. It's not a great oil-producing nation, yet you can't read a newspaper or newsmagazine or listen to the news without some reference to what's going on in that tiny piece of real estate. Why all the fuss over Israel?

The answer to this question is really quite simple: Israel is the eye of the hurricane of the great events of the end times. She is at the heart of most of the biblical prophecies for the end times. She occupies center stage in God's drama of the ages.

Here are the main biblical prophecies related to Israel's place in the end times.

1. Israel will be regathered and formed into a nation (see Isaiah 43:5–6; Jeremiah 30:3; Ezekiel 34:11–13; 37:1–14). Preparation for this began in May 1948 and continues up to the present. Almost half of the Jews worldwide are now back in the land of Israel.

2. The Antichrist will make a seven-year covenant of peace with Israel (see Daniel 9:27).

3. The Jewish people will rebuild the temple in Jerusalem (see Matthew 24:15).

4. Russia and her Islamic allies will invade the nation of Israel when she is at peace (see Ezekiel 38–39). (This invasion will be discussed in detail in the next chapter.)

5. The Antichrist will invade Israel and desecrate the temple (see Daniel 11:40–41; Matthew 24:15–20).

6. Many Jews will flee into the wilderness (see Revelation 12:13–17).

7. During the Tribulation, two-thirds of the Jews will perish (see Zechariah 13:8).

8. The armies of the world will gather in northern Israel at Megiddo (see Revelation 16:12–16).

9. Jerusalem will be attacked and taken (see Zechariah 12:1–9; 14:1–2).

10. Jesus Christ will return from heaven to defeat the armies of the world that will have gathered in Israel (see Revelation 19:19–21).

Israel is God's supersign of the end times.

ISRAEL AGAINST THE WORLD

One of the main prophecies concerning Israel in the end times is that Israel will be hated by the nations of the earth. The Bible presents the Tribulation as a time of mounting opposition against Israel, climaxing in an attack by all the nations of the earth.

"Behold, I am going to make Jerusalem a cup that causes reeling to all the peoples around; and when the siege is against Jerusalem, it will also be against Judah. It will come about in that day that I will make Jerusalem a heavy stone for all the peoples; all who lift it will be severely injured. And all the nations of the earth will be gathered against it." (Zechariah 12:2–3)

These verses are saying that the nations will be intoxicated with possessing the city of Jerusalem, but those who try to drink of it will face disaster. Israel will be a heavy, jagged stone that will cut to pieces those who try to remove her from her place.

You can see the frustration and hatred toward Israel growing in our world today. But what is behind it? Why has Israel been under constant threat of attack since the birth of the modern Israeli nation in 1948?

SATAN AND SEPTEMBER 11

One night during the week after the September 11 attack, I was watching *Fox News*. Brit Hume and his guest were talking about the horror of the attacks. At one point, Hume said something like, "The evil nature of this attack may cause many people to begin to think again about the reality of Satan."

I nearly fell out of my chair. I couldn't believe what I was hearing. The news anchor on *Fox News* was talking about Satan's role in the terrorist attack. I never thought I would hear Satan's role in world events discussed on prime-time news. The conversation went on for several minutes as they exchanged ideas concerning what people might conclude about Satan's part in the September 11 attacks.

This raises a very important point: According to Scripture, the real source of the opposition against Israel is not prejudice, but Satan. Revelation 12 pulls back the veil and shows us the real power behind all anti-Semitism. The Bible says that Satan is the archenemy of the Jewish people and of Jesus, their Messiah.

Ever since God promised Abraham that the Messiah would come through his lineage, Satan was on a mission to destroy Abraham's descendants, the Jewish people, to prevent the Messiah from coming. Satan instigated several unsuccessful attempts to eradicate the Jewish people. First, in about 480 B.C., Haman tried to wipe out the Jews in the days of

Esther. Second, in about 165 B.C., the Syrian monarch Antiochus Epiphanes tried to destroy them.

When he failed to prevent Messiah from coming—plan *A*—Satan then went to plan *B,* which was to kill Christ after He'd been born. Satan tried to destroy Him right after His birth through the evil of King Herod (see Matthew 2:13–18, Revelation 12:1–5). When this failed, he inspired the Jewish and Roman leaders to kill the Son of God. However, he failed to factor in the resurrection of Christ.

Now Satan is on plan *C.* Since he couldn't prevent Messiah from coming or kill Him and keep Him dead, his present goal is to destroy the Jewish people over whom the Messiah is to rule. Satan made his greatest attempt to destroy the Jewish people under the Third Reich. Adolf Hitler sent 6 million Jews to their deaths during his reign of terror.

In the end times, the Antichrist will begin his career by acting like he is the great friend of Israel, but in the Great Tribulation, he will slaughter the Jews mercilessly (see Daniel 7:25; 8:24; 11:44). The Antichrist will be totally empowered, controlled, and motivated by Satan. Therefore, his persecution of

Israel will be an expression of Satan's hatred for Israel.

I certainly don't profess to know all that was behind the attack on our nation on September 11, but I think we can safely say two things. First, the sovereign God of the universe allowed the events to take place as part of His perfect plan for this world. Second, since Satan is the avowed enemy of Israel and the U.S. is her chief ally and benefactor, it makes sense that Satan would inspire terrorists who hate Israel to spew out their venom against America.

So I agree with those who say that Satan had a major hand in what happened on September 11. No, his face didn't appear in the smoke, but we can certainly trace his hand in the flames. God loves Israel, but Satan hates her and anyone who supports her. As the time of the end draws near, Satan is stepping up his efforts to destroy Israel before his time runs out. Attacking America seems to be an integral part of that plan.

KEEP YOUR EYES ON ISRAEL

Israel is being mentioned everywhere today, it seems. She is back in her land just as the Bible predicts. She dominates world news. She is at the heart of peace in the Middle East. She is at the heart of world peace. And America's support for Israel was the cause of the most tragic day in our nation's history.

It all fits God's prophetic outline given to us in the Bible. Israel is God's supersign. So what is this supersign telling us now? If we view Israel as a kind of prophetic meter or gauge of where we are in God's prophetic program, I think we have to say that all indications are that the coming of Christ could be very near.

THE COMING ISLAMIC INVASION OF ISRAEL

"MASSIVE ISLAMIC CONFEDERATION
INVADES ISRAEL"
"RUSSIA LEADS ARAB ASSAULT FORCE
INTO ISRAEL"
"ISRAEL UNDER ATTACK FROM ALL SIDES"

An Arab-Islamic invasion of Israel is not too difficult to imagine today, is it? In fact, it's already happened several times in the past fifty years. Arab nations surrounding Israel have mounted furious attacks to eradicate the Jews, most recently in 1967 and 1973, only to be repelled and humiliated by the smaller Israeli army. Every Arab nation except Egypt and Jordan is in a declared state of war with

Israel right now, and those two could turn on Israel at any moment.

With every passing day, Arab-Islamic frustration with Israel grows. Israel controls land formerly under Muslim control. Jerusalem, the place from which Muhammad supposedly leaped to heaven, is Islam's third most holy site, after Mecca and Medina. Then there's the persistent Palestinian problem. Add to that the extremist Islamic states whose stated mission is to drive the Jews into the sea, and it's not too difficult to imagine another Arab-Islamic invasion of Israel in the near future.

The current situation is what we might call a "recipe for Middle-East turmoil." Let's look at the baking instructions:

- Take one land (Israel) and try to divide it into two equal parts. Set aside the section labeled "to the Arabs," but don't do anything with it yet.
- Add in the growth of radical Muslim extremism.
- Add in a pinch of Saddam Hussein, Muammar Qaddafi, and Arab terrorism.

- Add one disintegrated former Soviet Union and the possible proliferation of nuclear technology.
- Mix well and let simmer until it explodes.[7]

ENTER EZEKIEL

Amazingly, this is exactly what the Bible predicts. Ezekiel 38–39 prophesies that a massive confederation of nations will invade the land of Israel while she is enjoying a time of great peace and prosperity. The prophet Ezekiel wrote these chapters over twenty-five hundred years ago, yet they read like today's headlines.

These chapters are up-to-date for three reasons. First, as we have already seen, Israel today is once again a sovereign nation, just as Ezekiel predicted.

Second, Ezekiel predicted that Israel would one day achieve the peace and prosperity she so desperately yearns for, although it will be a pseudopeace that won't last long. Great efforts are currently underway in the United States and Europe to bring about a solution for the Israeli-Palestinian problem, thus ensuring peace for the region. Ezekiel foresaw a day in which this would occur.

Third, over twenty-five hundred years ago, Ezekiel specifically listed the precise alliance of nations that will invade Israel in the latter years or end times:

And the word of the LORD came to me saying, "Son of man, set your face toward Gog of the land of Magog, the prince of Rosh, Meshech and Tubal, and prophesy against him and say, 'Thus says the Lord GOD, "Behold, I am against you, O Gog, prince of Rosh, Meshech and Tubal. I will turn you about and put hooks into your jaws, and I will bring you out, and all your army, horses and horsemen, all of them splendidly attired, a great company with buckler and shield, all of them wielding swords; Persia, Ethiopia and Put with them, all of them with shield and helmet; Gomer with all its troops; Beth-togarmah from the remote parts of the north with all its troops—many peoples with you."'" (Ezekiel 38:1–6)

You might be shocked to know the identity of these invading nations. The names Ezekiel used were the ancient geographical names that existed in his day, but when we look at the countries that hold these areas today, we discover that it reads like a who's who list of Israel's current enemies.

Here are the nine specific geographical locations listed in Ezekiel 38:1–6:

ANCIENT NAME	MODERN NATION	EXPLANATION
Rosh	Russia	Ancient Sarmatians—known as Rashu, Rasapu, Ros, and Rus.
Magog	Central Asia	Ancient Scythians—Islamic southern republics of the former Soviet Union with a population of 60 million Muslims. This territory could include modern Afghanistan.
Meshech	Turkey	Ancient Muschki and Musku in Cilicia and Cappadocia.
Tubal	Turkey	Ancient Tubalu in Cappadocia.
Persia	Iran in 1935	Name changed from Persia to Iran.
Ethiopia	Sudan	Ancient Cush, south of Egypt.
Libya	Libya	Ancient Put, west of Egypt.
Gomer	Turkey	Ancient Cimmerians—from the seventh century to first century B.C. in central/western Anatolia.
Beth-togarmah	Turkey	Til-garimmu—between ancient Carchemish and Haran (southern Turkey).

From this list it is clear that at least six key allies will come together for this invasion: Russia, Turkey, Iran, Libya, Sudan, and the nations of Central Asia. Amazingly, all of these nations except Russia are Muslim nations. What's more, Iran, Libya, and Sudan are three of Israel's most ardent opponents *and* are listed by the U.S. government as states that support terrorism. Many of these nations are either forming or strengthening their ties as these words are being written. It's not too difficult to imagine these nations conspiring together to invade Israel in the near future.

Ezekiel prophesied that these nations, led by Russia, will come against Israel in the last days, at a time when the people of Israel are living in peace and prosperity (see Ezekiel 38:8–12). This probably describes the first half of the Tribulation, when Israel will be living under her peace treaty with the Antichrist. Near the middle of the Tribulation, Russia and her Islamic allies will descend upon the nation of Israel "like a storm and cover the land like a cloud" (v. 9, NLT).

There are four main reasons why Russia and her Islamic allies will invade Israel:

1. to cash in on the wealth of Israel (see Ezekiel 38:11–12),
2. to control the Middle East,
3. to crush Israel,
4. and to challenge the authority of Antichrist (see Daniel 11:40–44).

Since Israel will at this time be under a peace treaty with the Antichrist, who will be the leader of the Western world, an attack against Israel by this Middle Eastern coalition would be a direct challenge to the Antichrist's authority.

What will happen when these nations invade Israel? The Bible is very clear: God Himself will intervene to destroy them (see Ezekiel 38:18–23). With the destruction of this major power bloc near the middle of the Tribulation, the Antichrist will seize the opportunity, invade Israel himself, invade North Africa, set up his headquarters in Jerusalem, and establish his worldwide empire virtually unopposed (see Daniel 11:40–45).

More to Come

The Islamic invasion of Israel is our second gauge for measuring the nearness of the end times, so what does the meter read today?

Well, Israel and Islam have been pushed front and center in the world due to the attacks on September 11. The Bible predicts that Israel and the alliance of these Islamic nations will be two of the major players in the end times, and that's exactly what we see today.

This invasion has not occurred yet. Indeed, it will not transpire until halfway through the Tribulation, which is three and a half years after the church is raptured. But the stage is certainly set for this attack to happen. Its shadow has already fallen over the world. I believe that we must conclude that this sign of the times could be near, making the Rapture even nearer still.

If modern Israel and the current alignment of these Islamic nations were the only two signs of the times surrounding us today, that would be enough to get our attention.

But there's more. Much more.

SIX

WAR AND PEACE

When I was growing up in the sixties and seventies, there were two great military powers in the world: the United States and the Soviet Union. Although the Soviet Union was a great menace, the presence of these two superpowers created a certain balance of power in the world.

We used to think that if the Soviet Union collapsed, the world would be a much safer place. Were we ever wrong! Since the dissolution of the Soviet Union in 1991, the world has become an increasingly more dangerous place. Sadly, a look at the world scene today makes the cold-war era look like the good ol' days.

There are no longer two key players in the balance-of-power formula—there seem to be dozens. The world is more at risk today for nuclear detonations and biological and chemical warfare than ever before. Pakistan and India have the bomb. So does China and probably North Korea. It's only a matter of time until rogue states, terrorists, or fanatics get their hands on these weapons of mass destruction. The unrest in key Islamic nations could easily erupt into an explosive call for widespread jihad, or holy war.

Our uncertain world today needs peace and safety. People the world over are clamoring for peace—peace in the Balkans, peace in strife-torn African nations, peace in America. But most of all, people seem to be clamoring for peace in the Middle East.

People are also yearning for safety. The world has become obsessed with security. We have never felt more unsafe, more exposed, or more vulnerable than we do right now. We want safety: safety for ourselves, safety for our children, safety from a nuclear nightmare, safety from terrorist bombings, safety from bioterrorism, and safety from chemical warfare. We want safe water, safe food, and safe air travel.

Of course, this longing is nothing new. But with the rise of war by stealth—the sudden, unexpected strike of terrorism—the cry for peace and safety has become a worldwide clamor.

Amazingly, the Bible predicts that someday the world will finally achieve peace *and* safety. Hard as it is for us to imagine, Scripture says that a day is coming when people everywhere will be saying, "All is well; everything is peaceful and secure" (1 Thessalonians 5:3, NLT).

How will this ever be achieved? Frankly, right now it looks impossible. But the Bible says a man is coming who will give the world what it clamors for and bring it to pass. The Bible calls this man the Antichrist.

MAN OF PEACE, MAN OF POWER

Most people don't realize that the Bible contains over one hundred passages that detail the origin, nationality, career, character, kingdom, and final doom of the Antichrist.

What do you think of when you hear the word

Antichrist? Maybe you see him as a crazed madman, a diabolical fiend, a modern Adolf Hitler, or a shameless egomaniac. All of these images are accurate, but none of them pictures what Antichrist will be like when the world gets its first impression of him.

At the beginning of his career, the Antichrist will come on the world scene insignificantly. The first clear mention of him in the Bible is in Daniel 7:8, where he is called a little horn. He will appear inconspicuous at first.

The first clue in Scripture about the identity of the Antichrist is found in Daniel 9:27, where he is pictured brokering a peace treaty with Israel: "And he will make a firm covenant with the many [Israel] for one week [seven years]." This means that the first glimpse the world gets of the Antichrist will be of a great peacemaker.

What is the exact nature of this covenant that Antichrist will make with Israel? Charles Dyer, a respected prophecy teacher and author, says:

What is this "covenant" that the Antichrist will make with Israel? Daniel does not specify its content, but he does indicate that it will extend for seven years. During the first half of this time Israel feels at peace and secure, so the covenant must provide some guarantee for Israel's national security. Very likely the covenant will allow Israel to be at peace with her Arab neighbors. One result of the covenant is that Israel will be allowed to rebuild her temple in Jerusalem. This world ruler will succeed where Kissinger, Carter, Reagan, Bush, and other world leaders have failed. He will be known as the man of peace![8]

The Antichrist will come with the olive branch in his hand. He will come on the scene and accomplish what was considered impossible: He will solve the Middle Eastern peace puzzle and rid the world of terrorism. He will be hailed as the greatest peacemaker who has ever lived.

You can just see it now. He will be *Time* magazine's Man of the Year; he will win the Nobel Peace Prize.

THE RIDER ON
THE WHITE HORSE

A further picture of the Antichrist's peaceful entrance onto the world stage is given in Revelation 6:2. Here the Antichrist is pictured as a rider on a white horse, a pseudo-Christ who will ride onto the world scene initially in the power of peace. "I looked, and behold, a white horse, and he who sat on it had a bow; and a crown was given to him, and he went out conquering and to conquer" (Revelation 6:2).

Notice that he wears a victor's crown and has a bow but no arrows. This seems to indicate that he will win a bloodless victory at the beginning of his career. The bow indicates the threat of war, but it never materializes because he is able to gain victory through peaceful negotiations.

He brings what the world wants more than anything else: worldwide peace and safety. We know that he ushers in a time of global peace because the rider on the second horse (the red horse of Revelation 6:3–4) comes and takes peace from the earth. For peace to be taken from the earth, it must first exist there.

SATANIC SUPERMAN

How will the Antichrist pull this off? How will he do what so many others have miserably failed to do? The answer is that he will be totally energized and empowered by Satan himself. He will have the full power of the evil one behind him like no other man who has ever lived. "And the dragon [Satan] gave him [the Antichrist] his power and his throne and great authority" (Revelation 13:2).

Thus the Antichrist will possess all the best qualities of all the great leaders who have ever lived, rolled into one man. To help us better envision what the Antichrist will be like, H. L. Willmington, a noted expert in Bible prophecy, has provided this helpful analogy with American presidents. The coming world ruler will possess:

- the leadership of a Washington and Lincoln,
- the eloquence of a Franklin Roosevelt,
- the charm of a Teddy Roosevelt,
- the charisma of a Kennedy,
- the popularity of an Ike,

- the political savvy of a Johnson, and
- the intellect of a Jefferson.[9]

Since the Antichrist will be uniquely empowered by Satan, he will at first masquerade as an angel of light like his master does, not yet revealing his true goal, which is world conquest. But at the midpoint of the Tribulation, the mask of peace will come off and the world will be plunged into the terrible darkness of the Great Tribulation.

SUDDEN DESTRUCTION

Man's utopia won't last long. God will interrupt the pseudopeace with the outpouring of His wrath and the outbreak of war. "While they are saying, 'Peace and safety!' then destruction will come upon them suddenly like labor pains upon a woman with child, and they will not escape" (1 Thessalonians 5:3).

When the rider on the red horse (see Revelation 6:3–4) gallops forth with a mighty sword in his hand, much of the world will be plunged into war and slaughter.

For once, Israel will be an island of peace while the

rest of the world is at war. She will continue to enjoy peace for the first three and a half years of the Tribulation until she is invaded by Russia and her Islamic allies, and then by Antichrist. But most of the world will begin to experience what Jesus predicted: "You will be hearing of wars and rumors of wars. See that you are not frightened, for those things must take place, but that is not yet the end. For nation will rise against nation, and kingdom against kingdom" (Matthew 24:6–7).

So much for man's ability to bring peace to the world.

A WAITING WORLD

If we use war and the outcry for peace as gauges for the nearness of the end times, what do these signs tell us? I believe we must conclude that the stage is fully set.

The same world that rejected the true Christ and hung Him on a cross is ripe for the rise of Antichrist. The world that rejected the Light of the World will gladly embrace the prince of darkness. The world that crucified the Prince of Peace will hail the beast out of the sea. The world that couldn't tolerate the presence of the Holy One will welcome the man of sin.

Why? Because man wants to run this world himself. Man wants to do things his own way—without God.

As the world becomes a more dangerous place with unseen, faceless enemies, people will clamor for someone who can bring peace and safety. We want peace. We want safety. We want the Middle East peace process to materialize. We want an end to terrorism. And the world is committed to make it happen. We are enamored with diplomatic negotiations, with coalitions and alliances. World leaders love to posture, plan, ponder, and propose, but usually with meager, momentary results.

However, a man is coming who will be able to get things done. He will be a man of action. A man of accomplishments. The world will welcome him with open arms. Then, ultimately, the world will fall at his feet and worship him as god.

And we can be sure that Satan will have his counterfeit Christ ready to spring into action when the time is right. Since Satan's goal is to rule over and be worshiped by the world, I believe that in every generation he has a man ready to bring onto the world scene and take control. In every generation he has *an* Antichrist ready to take over when the time is right. So we can be sure that he has a man somewhere on the scene *right now,* waiting in the wings to give the world what it wants.

Who knows? *The* Antichrist may be waiting in the wings right now.

THE RUSH
TOWARD GLOBALISM

The Bible says that after the flood of the earth recorded in Genesis, all the people of the world congregated at one location under the leadership of one man, Nimrod, to build a great tower to the heavens (see Genesis 10:8–10; 11:1–9). The whole world was one community in a global rebellion against its Creator. Knowing the inherent danger of all the people being in one group, God confounded the language of man, thus dispersing the rebel race over the face of the earth.

Ever since that time, Satan has tried in vain to again bring the world under the control of one man through whom he could rule all. He tried with the Pharaohs, Nebuchadnezzar, Alexander the Great, the Caesars, Napoleon, and Hitler.

The Bible predicts that in the end times the world will once again come together in a one-world economy, government, and religion and that mankind will shake its collective fist in the face of the Creator. The Antichrist will lead this global revolution (see Revelation 13:3–18).

Until recently it would have been impossible to rule the entire world and control the world economy. Ancient rulers could have ruled the known world, perhaps, but their reign could not extend to every people under the sun. But all that has changed dramatically, especially in the last ten years.

The 1990s have been called the decade of globalization. Incredible developments have occurred that have advanced globalization at warp speed. Here are just a few of the main contributors:

- the end of the cold war,
- the creation of the World Trade Organization,
- the advance of the Internet, and

- the establishment of world news agencies, particularly CNN.

A world that seemed so large and hopelessly fragmented only a few decades ago now seems small and interconnected. The world has shrunk from XXL to XXS almost overnight.

IT'S A SMALL WORLD AFTER ALL

Many of the events that have occurred in the wake of the terrorist attacks on September 11 highlight how we have become a global community. They reveal just how small and interconnected the world has become, both politically and economically.

Do you remember what happened in the European and Asian economic markets on September 12? They fell substantially. Why? Because the world economy is inextricably linked together. What happens in one region on the economic front has a profound ripple effect throughout the rest of the world.

Immediately after the attacks, leaders from all over the world called President Bush to offer their condolences and support. I couldn't believe what I was seeing and hearing. Russia was offering support and help. China offered condolences. Even Yasser Arafat condemned the attacks and offered his support.

Another thing that has occurred in recent years to bring the world together is the forming of worldwide coalitions to fight a common enemy. The first example of this occurred in the early part of the 1990s when the United States galvanized an impressive coalition of nations to support the war against Saddam Hussein, who had invaded Kuwait.

We have witnessed the same thing in the wake of September 11, 2001. Almost immediately after the terrorist attacks, President Bush and his top advisers were making calls to leaders all over the world to build a new coalition. Pakistan, a nation with very strained relations with the U.S., even allowed the use of its airspace to launch attacks against the Taliban in Afghanistan.

A worldwide coalition made up of some very strange bedfellows was coming together right before our eyes. It seemed like everyone wanted to be a part of this alliance. Only a few rogue states refused to join the team.

I don't believe all of this worldwide coalition

building is an accident or simply a coincidence. I believe it is part of a well-orchestrated plan. Not surprisingly, it is exactly the picture of the end of the age presented in Scripture.

FEET OF IRON AND CLAY

What we are witnessing on a worldwide scale is also seen most graphically in the West. Scripture predicts, in passages like Daniel 2 and 7, that world power in the end times will be concentrated in the reunited Roman Empire—what we know today as Europe or the Western world. The fifteen nations of the European Union (EU) seem to be the precursor to the ten-kingdom form of the reunited Roman Empire predicted in Daniel. After sixteen centuries of division, the nations of Europe are back together again.

The EU went to one unified currency, the Euro, in January 2002. Now that these nations all have the same currency, there will be no turning back. They will be linked together with an unbreakable bond. The Roman Empire is being reunited and revived right before our eyes, just as Daniel predicted twenty-five hundred years ago!

Not only are the nations of Europe coming together among themselves, but the attack on September 11 is galvanizing the alliance between the United States and those European nations. For the first time in fifty-two years, the clause of mutual defense and protection in the NATO treaty came into effect.

Who is the main U.S. ally in the war on terror? Europe. The U.S. is probably closer to her European allies right now than at any time I can remember. This closing of ranks will no doubt be magnified when the Rapture occurs. America, losing millions of citizens at the Rapture, will probably join with Europe at that time to form the great Western confederacy of the end times.

ONE WORLD
UNDER ANTICHRIST

Two thousand years ago, the apostle John predicted exactly what we see developing before our eyes today—a global community focused in the Western world, headed by one man (see Revelation 13). The events of September 11 have given this already strong movement a hard push downstream. The Roman Empire is being reunited right before our eyes. And the United States, the world's only true superpower, seems ready and willing to join forces with the new global community.

Today, the idea of a one-world government and economy no longer seems far-fetched or bizarre. In fact, it seems like the natural result of the trends we see all around us.

I think we would have to conclude that this end-times gauge, too, is telling us that the time could be near. The rush toward globalism is just another way the stage is being set for one man to come on the scene and rule the entire world for three and a half years, just as the Bible predicts.

MOVING TOWARD THE MARK

It didn't take very long. I expected it and it came. Only a couple of weeks after the attack on America, serious talk began of a national ID card for all American citizens. This is an amazing development.

The new ID card would contain your photograph and have your thumbprint digitized and embedded right on the card. Millions of American would be fingerprinted, and that information would be placed in a huge database that airport security officials or law enforcement agencies could use.

Here's how it would work. When you went into an airport, you would simply place the card in a reader, put your thumb down, and wait for the system to confirm your identity.

Is this really possible? Oracle chairman and CEO Larry Ellison called for this national identification card system only eleven days after the terrorist attacks. And he is willing to put his money where his mouth is. Ellison, who is worth $15 billion, is willing to *donate* the software to make this system a reality.

Responding to charges that this ID card would be an invasion of privacy, Ellison said:

> Well, this privacy you're concerned about is largely an illusion. All you have to give up is your illusions, not any of your privacy. Right now, you can go on to the Internet and get a credit report about your neighbor and find out where your neighbor works, how much they earn and if they had a late mortgage payment and tons of other information.[10]

BRAVE NEW WORLD

The thing that is so eerie about so many of these recent developments in the wake of the terrorist attack is that they seem so natural. They seem like the right things to do. It seems right for the world to come together against terror. It seems right and natural to many leaders to implement a national ID card as an option in the fight against terrorism. As House Democratic Leader Richard Gephardt said, "We are in a new world. This event will change the balance between freedom and security."

I was amazed to see the results of a survey by the Pew Research Center for the People and the Press on September 19, 2001. It said that *seven out of ten* Americans favored a requirement that citizens carry a national identity card at all times to show to a police officer upon request. Women particularly showed strong support for this proposal.

A *Reader's Digest* poll entitled "How Much Freedom Would You Give Up?" found that 70 percent of Americans surveyed responded "Yes" to a proposal to "establish a national registration of digital identity checks, such as fingerprints or eye scans."[11]

In an effort to tighten security at sensitive buildings, including the Pentagon, the U.S. Department of Defense has ordered chip-based ID cards ("smart cards") for 4.3 million military personnel over the next eighteen months. These "common access cards" are about the size of a credit card and will replace the green ID cards now used by Department of Defense employees. The cards will be required to open secure doors, get cash, buy food, and check out weapons and ammunition.

ID cards may eventually be issued to more of the 23 million individuals in the Department of Defense's database, including family members, retired servicemen, and contractors. Many view the adoption of these cards by the military as laying the groundwork for the introduction of national ID cards in the U.S.

Tony Blair, the prime minister of Great Britain, has tentatively approved identity cards to be introduced there on a voluntary basis. However, the card may not be so voluntary after all since it may be required to board an aircraft, buy gas, open a bank account, begin a new job, or claim government benefits.

In a nationwide poll of British citizens released on September 23, 2001, a stunning 85 percent said they would welcome a national ID card system. A vast majority want the card packed with information that would clearly identify the cardholder, such as a photograph, date of birth, eye color, a fingerprint, DNA details, criminal record, and religion.

According to British government officials, they have no plans to introduce legislation on ID cards in the near future, but there seems to be a growing movement in favor of this new method of fighting terrorism. British Home Secretary David Blunkett has said that the government is "very seriously" considering introducing a card and that he is giving it a "fairly high priority."

BIG BROTHER

The national ID card has been pushed to the forefront of national discussion by the attacks on the World Trade Center and the Pentagon. This is another way that the events of September 11 have had a major stage-setting impact.

The Bible predicts that when the Antichrist comes on the world scene, he will rule over a one-world economy, a one-world government, and a one-world religion (see Revelation 13:1–18). One of the key components of his world control will be the ability to control world commerce by requiring that every person receive Antichrist's mark on either his right hand or his forehead in order to buy or sell anything (see Revelation 13:16–18).

The word *mark* refers to a brand or tattoo. It signifies loyalty, ownership, or protection. The technology is now readily available to tattoo, brand, or embed a number on or under the skin of every person alive to regulate world commerce and security.

Henry Morris, an expert in Bible prophecy, observes:

> The nature of the mark is not described, but the basic principle has been established for years in various nations. The social security card, the draft registration card, the practice of stenciling an inked design on the back of the hand, and various other devices are all forerunners of this universal branding. The word itself ("mark") is the Greek *charagma*. It is used only in Revelation, to refer to the mark of the beast (eight times), plus one time to refer to

idols "graven by art and man's device" (Acts 17:29). The mark is something like an etching or a tattoo which, once inscribed, cannot be removed, providing a permanent (possibly eternal) identification as a follower of the beast and the dragon.[12]

On December 12, 2001, just three months after the terrorist attacks, the United States and Canada signed a border security agreement that would provide a "smart border" between the two nations. The agreement calls for the use of so-called biometric identifiers—fingerprints, voice recognition, or retinal scans—in travel documents to make it easier to identify people who've been cleared through a screening process. "Travelers who 'pose no risk' would be 'speeded along their way.'"[13]

It is not difficult to imagine the use of such a technology, or even of a national identification card adopted in the U.S. and England, spreading to all of Europe and then the world. The presence of this universally accepted practice and technology would be easily adapted by the Antichrist, who will arise out of

Europe (the reunited Roman Empire), to function as a worldwide identification system for his followers.

WAIT AND SEE

We don't know exactly what technology or technique will be used by the Antichrist to identify his followers. We will have to wait and see how the current developments in this area continue to unfold in the coming days, but it seems that another piece of the stage furniture has been put in place for the final drama of the ages.

The frightening thing is that the events of September 11 have made such a system seem right and natural. Even desirable.

ARE YOU READY?

In 1974, John Walvoord wrote his bestselling book *Oil, Armageddon and Middle East Crisis,* which was later reprinted during the Gulf War crisis. His words are more timely today than when he wrote them:

> The world is like a stage being set for a great drama. The major actors are already in the wings waiting for their moment in history. The main props are already in place. The prophetic play is about to begin. The Middle East today occupies the attention of world

leaders. The world has now recognized the political and economic power in the hands of those who control the tremendous oil reserves of the area. Old friendships and alliances will be subject to change as European nations seek new alliances and agreements to protect themselves in a changing world situation. The Middle East will continue to be the focal point of international relationships.

All the necessary historical developments have already taken place. The trend toward world government, begun with the United Nations in 1946, is preparing the way for the government of the end time.

Israel and the nations of the world have been prepared for the final drama. Most important, Israel is back in the land, organized as a political state, and eager for her role in the end-time events. Today Israel desperately needs the covenant of peace promised in prophecy. Largely because of the demands of the Palestinians, Israel will not be able to achieve a satisfactory settlement in direct negotiations.[14]

Walvoord notes how Russia seems to be poised to the north of Israel for entry in the end-time conflict, then he says:

> Egypt and other African countries have not abandoned their desire to attack Israel from the south. Red China in the east is now a military power great enough to field an army as large as that described in the book of Revelation. Each nation is prepared to play out its role in the final hours of history.
>
> Our present world is well prepared for the beginning of the prophetic drama that will lead to Armageddon. Since the stage is being set for this dramatic climax of the age, it must mean that Christ's coming for His own is very near. If there ever was an hour when men should consider their personal relationship to Jesus Christ, it is today. God is saying to this generation: "Prepare for the coming of the Lord."[15]

Never before in human history has there been such a convergence of trends and developments that are part of the matrix of end-time events predicted in Scripture. Below are six of the most important gauges we have been reading. What they are telling us ought to grab our attention.

1. Israel is back in her land as a nation, after a nineteen-hundred-year absence, and she is a jagged, heavy burden to the world—an unsolvable problem for the world's diplomats.

2. The Islamic alliance of nations predicted in Ezekiel 38 is in place.

3. The Roman Empire, after being divided for sixteen hundred years, is being reunited with the rise of the European Union. The permanent move to one currency in 2002 has welded much of Europe together into an inseparable whole.

4. The speed at which the world is becoming a global community is staggering.

5. The world today is a more dangerous place than ever before. The worldwide cry for peace and safety is deafening. Our world is ripe for a

charismatic peacemaker to burst onto the
world scene to bring peace on earth.

6. The rapid development and availability of
technology and the one-world economy make
the fulfillment of the mark of the beast seem
more like a future fact than science fiction.

In light of all these signs, we have to conclude that it's
later than it has ever been before! The timing of the end
times is known only by God, but from a human stand-
point, it appears that all the pieces of the puzzle are
falling into place. The time may be very short. Indeed,
the truth is that none of us knows how much time we
have, either *personally* or *prophetically*.

Personally, we don't know if we will live to see
tomorrow. God gives us no guarantee of another
breath. Prophetically, Jesus could come today, and all
who don't know Him will be left behind.

The signs of the end are all around us. Though
many people are searching for answers, most are ignoring God's warnings.

REMEMBER HARRY TRUMAN

In his book *Approaching Hoofbeats,* Billy Graham relates this fascinating story about the importance of heeding the warning signs God has given us.

Mt. Saint Helens belched gray steam plumes hundreds of feet into the blue Oregon sky. Geologists watched their seismographs in growing wonder as the earth danced beneath their feet. Rangers and state police, sirens blaring, herded tourists and residents from an ever-widening zone of danger. Every piece of scientific evidence being collected in the laboratories and on the field predicted the volcano would soon explode with a fury that would leave the forests flattened.

"Warning!" blared loudspeakers on patrol cars and helicopters hovering overhead. "Warning!" blinked battery powered signs at every major crossroad. "Warning!" pleaded radio and television announcers, shortwave and citizens-band operators. "Warning!" echoed up and down the mountain; and lakeside villages, tourist camps and hiking trails emptied as people heard the warnings and fled for their lives.

But Harry Truman refused to budge. Harry was the caretaker of a recreation lodge on Spirit Lake, five miles north of Mt. Saint Helen's smoke-enshrouded peak. The rangers warned Harry of the coming blast. Neighbors begged him to join them in their exodus. Even Harry's sister called to talk sense into the old man's head. But Harry ignored the warnings. From the picture-postcard beauty of his lakeside home reflecting the snow-capped peak overhead, Harry grinned on national television and said, "Nobody knows more about this mountain than Harry and it don't dare blow up on him."[16]

But the volcano proved him wrong. Graham tells it this way:

On 18 May 1980, as the boiling gases beneath the mountain's surface bulged and buckled the landscape to its final limits, Harry Truman cooked his eggs and bacon, fed his sixteen cats the scraps, and began to plant petunias around the border of his freshly mowed lawn. At 8:31 A.M. the mountain exploded.

Did Harry regret his decision in that millisecond he had before the concussive waves, traveling faster than the speed of sound, flattened him and everything else for 150 square miles? Did he struggle against the wall of mud and ash fifty feet high that buried his cabin, his cats and his freshly mowed law—or had he been vaporized (like 100,000 people at Hiroshima) when the mountain erupted with a force 500 times greater than the nuclear bomb which leveled that Japanese city?

Now Harry is a legend in the corner of [Washington] where he refused to listen. He smiles down on us from posters and T-shirts and beer mugs. Balladeers sing a song about old Harry, the stubborn man who put his ear to the mountain but would not heed its warnings.[17]

Billy Graham concludes the story with these thought-provoking words: "Maybe you are like ol' Harry Truman today. You see the warning signs all around you, yet you are ignoring them. You are going on with your life."[18]

This may describe you right now. You see the signs all around you, but you are trying to ignore them. You are going on with your life. If so, then the most important thing for you to do is to hear God's Word and be saved from the wrath to come.

WHAT MUST I DO TO BE SAVED?

Are you ready to meet the Lord? You can be. The Lord's plan for saving man from His sins is so easy that the Bible says we must become like a little child to enter God's kingdom.

Becoming a child of God involves three important steps: admit, acknowledge, and accept.

Step 1: Admit

You must realize that you need to be saved. You must admit your need. How many sins did it take for

Adam and Eve to be excluded forever from the Garden of Eden? Just one. Likewise, it takes only one sin to keep us out of God's heaven. And if we are honest, we know that all of us have committed many sins against the Lord. Romans 3:23 tells the truth about us: "For all have sinned and fall short of the glory of God."

Step 2: Acknowledge

You must acknowledge that you need a Savior. You cannot save yourself. No amount of good works, effort, church attendance, or ritual can take away your sin. "For by grace you have been saved through faith; and that not of yourselves, it is the gift of God; not as a result of works, so that no one may boast" (Ephesians 2:8–9).

Step 3: Accept

You must receive or accept Jesus Christ as your personal Savior from sin. It's not enough just to know that you are a sinner and that you need a Savior. You must acknowledge that Jesus is the Savior you need, that He died on the cross to take away your sins, and that He rose again on the third day. And you must receive Him by faith. You must take the free gift of eternal life that God offers. "But as many as received Him, to them He gave the right to become children of God, even to those who believe in His name" (John 1:12).

TODAY IS THE DAY OF SALVATION

Why not bow your head right now and call upon the Lord, accepting Christ as your personal Savior? Do it now. Don't put it off. It will be the greatest decision you will ever make. When you receive Christ, God promises to give you the precious gift of eternal life: "He who believes in the Son has eternal life" (John 3:36a). If you want to get ready for Jesus' return but you don't know Him as Lord and Savior, then this is what you need to do to prepare for His coming.

GRACE LIVING

If you have just received Christ or if you have been a Christian for some time, you need to thank God again for His gracious gift of salvation and for calling you out of darkness into His marvelous light.

"Thank God for his Son—a gift too wonderful for words!" (2 Corinthians 9:15, NLT).

In thankful response to God's grace, you need to live in such a way that you are ready for the Lord to come at any moment. Here are seven practical ways to stay alert and be ready:

1. If you have never followed the Lord in believer's baptism, then you need to obey the Lord's command to be baptized in water (see Matthew 28:19).
2. Put away any known sin in your life. Turn from it today. Ask for God's help to do it. Commit to being a pure vessel for the Lord to use (see 2 Timothy 2:20–22).
3. Confess any known sin in your life so you can be restored in fellowship with the Lord (see 1 John 1:9).
4. Keep the lines of communication open between you and your heavenly Father; pray daily (see 1 Thessalonians 5:17).
5. Find a loving, Bible-teaching church to attend, support, and serve in (see Hebrews 10:25).

6. Use the gifts and abilities the Lord has given you to serve others (see Matthew 25:14–30).
7. Look for Christ's coming each day (see Titus 2:13).

My prayer is that you will be ready when the midnight hour comes, because it's later than it has ever been before.

Multnomah Publishers
The publisher and author would love to hear your comments about this book. *Please contact us at:*
www.multnomah.net/hitchcock

NOTES

1. Billy Graham, *Till Armageddon* (Minneapolis, Minn.: Grason, 1981), 7.
2. Charles Caldwell Ryrie, *The Best Is Yet to Come,* (Chicago: Moody Press, 1981), 17–8.
3. Charles Caldwell Ryrie, *Revelation* (Chicago: Moody Press, 1968), 62.
4. Thomas Ice and Timothy Demy, *The Truth about the Signs of the Times* (Eugene, Ore.: Harvest House Publishers, 1997), 10–1.
5. Lisa Beyer, "Roots of Rage," *Time,* 1 October 2001, 45.
6. Scott Macleod, "A Royal Ruckus," *Time Europe,* 22 October, 2001, n.p.
7. Charles H. Dyer, *World News and Bible Prophecy* (Wheaton, Ill.: Tyndale, 1995), 100.
8. Ibid., 214.
9. H. L. Willmington, *The King Is Coming* (Wheaton, Ill.: Tyndale, 1973), 95.
10. Paul Rogers and Elise Ackerman, "Oracle Boss Urges National ID Cards, Offers Free Software," *San Jose Mercury News,* 22 September 2001.
11. "How Much Freedom Would You Give Up?" *Reader's Digest,* November 2001, 14.
12. Henry M. Morris, *The Revelation Record* (Wheaton, Ill.: Tyndale, 1983), 252.
13. "U.S., Canada Sign 'Smart Border' Declaration," *CNN.com,* 13 December 2001. http://www.cnn.com/2001/US/12/12/rec.canada.border/index.html (accessed 13 December 2001).
14. John Walvoord, *Oil, Armageddon and Middle East Crisis* (Grand Rapids, Mich.: Zondervan, 1990), 227–8.
15. Ibid.
16. Billy Graham, *Approaching Hoofbeats: The Four Horsemen of the Apocalypse* (Waco, Tex.: Word Books, 1983), 13–4.
17. Ibid.
18. Ibid., 14.

"The End Is Near!"

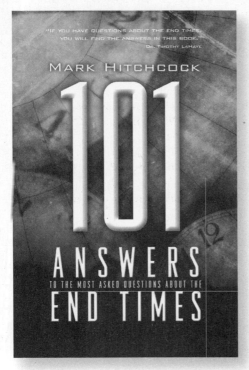

"Mark's newest book fills a real need in the study of prophecy. Finally, there's one book that gives solid, biblical answers to all the key questions that people today are asking about the End Times."

—DR. TIMOTHY LAHAYE

Or is it? The Antichrist is alive and well today! *Or is he?* The church is about to be raptured and will certainly escape the Tribulation....*right?* When it comes to the End Times, there's so much confusion. Preachers with elaborate charts share their theories about Revelation and other prophetic books of the Bible. "Ah, Babylon stands for the United States," they say. But then other teachers share their theories: "No, Babylon stands for the Roman Catholic Church, or the European Union, or the literal Babylon rebuilt in Iraq...." *Would somebody please shoot straight with me?* Finally, someone has. Gifted scholar and pastor Mark Hitchcock walks you gently through Bible prophecy in an engaging, user-friendly style. Hitchcock's careful examination of the topic will leave you feeling informed and balanced in your understanding of events to come...in our time?

ISBN 1-57673-952-X

Hitchcock Examines Bible prophecy's silence about America

In *Is America in Bible Prophecy?*, expert Mark Hitchcock deals with often-raised questions about America's future. Examining three prophetic passages that are commonly thought to describe America, Hitchcock concludes that the Bible is actually silent about the role of the United States in the End Times. He then discusses the implications of America's absence in prophetic writings. Along with Hitchcock's compelling forecast for the future, he offers specific actions Americans can take to keep their nation strong and blessed by God, as well as an appendix of additional questions and answers.

ISBN 1-57673-496-X